MMA Champions Training

The 7 Day Bootcamp To MASTERING the MMA Fundamentals

Greg Johnson

©2015 Greg Johnson

Copyright

© Copyright MMA Champions Training 2015 - All rights reserved.

This document is geared towards providing exact and reliable information in regards to the topic and issue covered. The publication is sold with the idea that the publisher is not required to render accounting, officially permitted, or otherwise, qualified services. If advice is necessary, legal or professional, a practiced individual in the profession should be ordered.

- From a Declaration of Principles which was accepted and approved equally by a Committee of the American Bar Association and a Committee of Publishers and Associations.

In no way is it legal to reproduce, duplicate, or transmit any part of this document in either electronic means or in printed format. Recording of this publication is strictly prohibited and any storage of this document is not allowed unless with written permission from the publisher. All rights reserved.

The information provided herein is stated to be truthful and consistent, in that any liability, in terms of inattention or otherwise, by any usage or abuse of any policies, processes, or directions contained within is the solitary and utter responsibility of the recipient reader. Under no circumstances will any legal responsibility or blame be held against the publisher for any reparation, damages, or monetary loss due to the information herein, either directly or indirectly.

Respective authors own all copyrights not held by the publisher.

The information herein is offered for informational purposes solely, and is universal as so. The presentation of the information is without contract or any type of guarantee assurance.

The trademarks that are used are without any consent, and the publication of the trademark is without permission or backing by the trademark owner. All trademarks and brands within this book are for clarifying purposes only and are the owned by the owners themselves, not affiliated with this document.

Table of Contents

INTRODUCTION

Chapter 1: Being Fit to Fight...

Chapter 2: Fighting Stance and Footwork...

Chapter 3: Striking Training...

Chapter 4: Take-downs & Take-down Defense...

Chapter 5: The Ground Game...

Chapter 6: The 7-Day MMA Boot Camp...

CONCLUSION

INTRODUCTION

Congratulations on your next step with *MMA Champions Training*.

This book contains proven steps and strategies on how to learn mixed martial art techniques from your own home.

MMA is not just a sport, but also a way of life. If you want to learn how to fight, you need to work on your body and mind every day. Mixed martial arts may be a physical sport but it requires you to be mentally fit as well. You need to develop the fighters mentality of attacking when the opportunity presents itself and to defend or evade when needed. You should also maintain an excellent level of fitness together with a well balanced diet.

Mixed martial arts require endurance and strength. Your cardio-respiratory health must be excellent to last 5 minutes in the fighting arena. You should also have strength behind your punches to do damage and you should be strong enough to resist your opponent's will. Lastly, you should have a good foundation in the fighting styles that dominate the sport. This book will help you develop these characteristics as you begin your journey in training to become a mixed martial arts fighter.

Thanks again for purchasing this book, I hope you enjoy it!

Greg

Chapter 1: Being Fit to Fight...

MMA is a very demanding sport. Even the training will burn out all your workout energy. You also need to be at your peak condition during fights as well as in sparring sessions.

To develop a body ready for fighting in 7 days, you need to start working out every day. This book assumes that you already do general workouts before starting this boot camp. We will only focus on fight-centered workouts.

Here are the specific fitness abilities that you need to develop and the workouts that you need to do to work on them:

Endurance

Accuracy

Speed and agility

Strength

Mixed martial art fighters need to last multiple rounds to win. If you are fighting with someone with the same level of skill, the determining factor will be your fitness. You see it time and again in the Octagon and other MMA arenas. The fighters fight to a stalemate for two straight rounds. You begin to see fatigue set in when the 3rd round starts. At the start of this round, one fighter stands from his chair with energy while the other is breathing heavily and waits until the referee's signal before standing up.

Whoever is more energetic wins ninety percent of the time.

You need to build your endurance to fight in the championship level. Championship fights in the UFC are five rounds long. Each round is 5 minutes long. You only have 1 minute of rest in between rounds. You should train your body to move around, do damage and defend for 25 minutes if you want to even survive against a UFC champion.

Luckily for you, endurance can be developed. Here is a 7-day training regimen if to develop this level of endurance:

Days 1,3 and 6

Jog for 15 minutes

Rest for 3 minutes before doing the next workout.

Sprints

   Do a sprint for 20 seconds straight. Take a 10-second rest in between reps. You should do 3 reps total.

Burpee with push-ups

   You start in a standing position. Bend your knees until your hands touch the floor, and then quickly extend your legs backward to the push-up position. Do two slow push-ups focusing on doing the correct form. Do the reverse actions to get back to the starting position. Do 5 reps of this exercise.

Muay Thai Knees

   Start by assuming a Thai Clinch Stance:

   Imagine that you have an opponent in front of you. Take your fighting stance. Right handed-fighters should take the orthodox fighting stance while left-handed fighters should take the southpaw stance. Put your jabbing hand on the back of your imaginary opponent's neck and your other hand over it. Do not interlock your fingers.

To start the rep raise you knee to strike your hands. Imagine hitting your imaginary opponent's lower jaw. Do 10 reps with each leg. Rest for 10 seconds and do another set. Do three sets to conclude the training.

The whole routine will last 50-60 minutes depending on your level of fitness. If you feel winded after this workout, you need to take a step back from the boot camp training and continue building your endurance.

Day 4: Rest Day

Day 2, 5 and 7:

Jog for 15 minutes

Rest for 3 minutes before doing the next workout.

Sprints

Do a sprint for 20 seconds straight. Take a 10-second rest in between reps. Do 5 reps totals.

Squats

Do 16 reps of squats within 1 minute. Rest for 30 seconds before doing it again. You should do five sets of this workout.

Jab-Straight Combination

The Jab-Straight combination is the most basic fist-striking move. It is a boxing move so you need to assume a boxing stance (orthodox or southpaw). Take a deep breath then throw a jab while blowing forcefully from your mouth and follow it with a straight punch with another strong blow from your mouth. To time your punches, count one-two as fast as you can in your mind as you are throwing them. Do as many jab-straight combinations as you can in 3 minutes.

You should increase the speed of your jab-straight combination as you do more workouts. If you feel that you are about to faint within or after the workout, you should stop immediately, rest and eat some crackers with water. If you feel like the workout is too hard or if you feel winded out with these routines, you should do more endurance training before moving on with the boot camp.

Chapter 2: Fighting Stance and Footwork...

The first thing that you need to do is to learn your fighting stance. In this aspect of the sport, we will borrow the stance used by boxers and modify it to make you more light on your feet.

For Right Handed Fighters

If you are a right-handed fighter, your power punch will come from your right hand. That means that your jabbing hand will be your left hand. The ideal stance for you is the orthodox stance. To do this stance, stand with your feet apart slightly wider than your shoulders. Clench your fists and bend your elbows to cover your lower jaw with your fists. Square yourself up against the opponent then take a step forward with your left foot. The foot should be pointing towards the direction of your opponent. Bend your torso so that your arms are covering your ribs. You should also twist your hips slightly so your torso is slightly facing your opponent. Lastly, bend your knees and widen the distance between your legs to achieve a lower center of gravity. Having bent knees will allow you to react better towards the opponents strikes.

For Left-handed Fighters

The opposite of the orthodox stance is the southpaw stance. In this position, the fighter's power punch comes from the left hand. To achieve this stance, use the same principles above but use the right legs and right arm as the lead.

Footwork

Forward movements

To move towards your opponent, take a small step with your lead leg and glide your rear leg to follow. You usually use this when attacking or when closing the distance between you and your opponent. To move diagonally to the right, use your right most leg to take a big step forward. Let your other leg follow to be able to get back to your stance. Use the same principle when moving forward diagonally to the left. Diagonal movements are used for increasing the reach of your attacks and to avoid power punches.

Backward movements

To move backwards, you should step first with your rear leg and glide your lead leg to the position that will allow you to get back to your fighting stance. If you need to take multiple steps backward, you could backpedal to do it faster. Backward movements are used to increase the distance between you and your opponent. This decreases the effectiveness of strikes.

Sidesteps

To sidestep, use the left leg to step first if you are moving to the left and use the opposite leg to move to the opposite direction. Make sure that you move the other leg fast to get back to your fighting stance as fast as you can. Sidesteps can also be used for both offense and defense. You can sidestep to evade enemy strikes without increasing the distance between you and your opponent, thus giving you a bigger chance for counter-attacking.

Chapter 3: Striking Training...

Striking in MMA refers to the act of throwing punches, kicks, knees or elbows at your opponent. Strikes that land on the head can knock out an opponent. In boxing, a well-placed left hook in the lower-right part of the opponent's ribs can cause unbearable pain that can immobilize him. It is also common for kicks and knees to the head to take out an opponent. Elbows on the other hand, create short blows to specific parts of the face that can open up wounds. Cuts in the eyebrows for instance can bleed towards the eye, which will lessen your opponent's vision. These are only some of the results that well-placed strikes can do. This chapter will help you develop the most effective striking attacks that you can immediately add to your offensive arsenal of skills.

Striking with the arms

You can do two types of strikes using your arms. You can throw punches and elbows towards an opponent. Let's start with punches.

In this book, we will discuss only five types of punches for you to learn. It doesn't matter how many punches you know. The important part is to know which type of strike to use in the right situation.

Jab

The jab is a type of punch done with the lead fist. Among the types of basic punches, jabs have the furthest reach. Because you jab with the forward-most fist, it can also reach the opponent faster than other types of punches. Because of the short distance of travel and the small amount of the fighter's weight behind the punch, the jab is weaker compared to the other punches. Jabs rarely knock out opponents; most fighters use jabs to rack up points and distract the opponents enough to set up stronger punches in the combination. It also used together with the footwork to measure the distance between you and the opponent without risking yourself of getting hit.

How to do it:

The first thing that you need to do is to take your fighting stance. You should then look at your target and focus on it. From your stance, push your lead leg and your lead arm simultaneously. From the fighting stance position, twist your arms slightly as you throw the punch to expose your two middle knuckles to your target. If your jab is too short to reach your target, go back to your original position by withdrawing your fist and moving your back leg forward to move you closer to your target. From this position, you should try the jab again to check the opponent's distance.

Straight and cross

The straight and cross are very similar punches. They are done with the rear arm of your stance. Often called power punches because, if done correctly, there is more weight behind the straight and cross.

How to do it:

From your fighting stance, extend your rear arm towards your opponent, pushing your lead shoulder back as you throw. Simultaneously, you should pivot your rear leg to extend the reach and also put more weight behind the punch. If you throw your lead elbow back further, you will increase your reach and that's what makes the right cross. Your lead fist should stay in front of your lower jaw for defense against the opponent's counter punch.

Use the straight if the opponents is close, and the cross if they are further back.

Hook

How to do it:

Lead fist

From your fighting stance, pull your lead shoulder back to prepare the punch, and then release your fist to the side of the body. Your whole torso should then turn to throw your fist. Your fist should make a circular motion from the side of your body towards your opponent's jaw. Pivot on your lead foot to give your punch more power. There are two ways to land the hook; one is with the thumb facing toward you, and the other with it facing upward. Experiment on which way you like better.

Rear fist

Use the same principle with the lead hook, but instead of pivoting your lead foot you use your other one.

Uppercut

The uppercut is a punch that targets the opponent's chin. Use this during close distances or if the opponent like to bend to low. In MMA, you can also throw uppercuts while clinching; this increases the chances of it hitting their intended mark.

How to do it:

From your fighting stance, lower your lead fist by bending your whole torso. Forcefully direct your fist upwards towards your opponent's head, chin or body by twisting your hips and your whole torso; the power of this punch comes from this rotation.

Hammer fist

The hammer fist is a short distance punch used in the ground in very short distances. It intends to attack the bridge of the nose or any open wound in the face.

How to do it:

Hit the opponent with the pinkie side of your fist, as if you were hammering down a nail.

Elbows strikes

For beginners, the most effective elbow strikes can come from the side or from below. They are more effective than punches in making damage when the opponent is too close for a punch. Aim it at the opponent's lips, nose or eyebrows. These areas are common places in the face where wounds start. They are also effective in the ground when the opponent is on his back.

Kicks and Knee Strikes

Kicks and knee strikes are also important skills to learn. By learning these fighting techniques, you will be able to throw more types of strikes in your combination; thus making you unpredictable. The only problem is that kicks consume more energy than punches. Relying on kicks and knee strikes may cause you to tire quickly. In addition, certain types of kicks like the roundhouse kick leaves you in a vulnerable position if you miss your target. Use high power, but risky, kicks like these in moderation.

Sidekicks

Sidekicks are the most commonly used kicks in MMA because they can thrown with power from a variety of angles. You should have this in your arsenal of skills because it is the foundation of more advanced types of kicks. To do a right side kick for orthodox fighters, take your fighting stance and lift your knees as close to your chest as possible with your toes pointing downward. Launch your leg to the side aiming to hit the enemy with the outer side of your foot. Position your arms properly to defend against counters and to maintain your balance. Your standing foot will automatically point towards opposite the direction of the kick to maintain your balance. Your torso will also bend slightly to achieve balance.

Back kick

A back kick is a variation of the sidekick, but you do this when the opponent is slightly behind you. Just like the sidekick, you start this move by raising your knees to your chest. Launch your legs directly towards a back target while bending your torso forward to maintain balance. You should end up with a position similar to the sidekick.

Spinning back kick and the roundhouse kick

These two are very powerful kicks that you can easily add to your arsenal of skills. They are both done with your rear leg. To do the spinning back kick, you pivot with your lead leg to make a turn allowing your rear leg to hit the opponent.

A roundhouse kick on the other hand is probably one of the most popular kicks around. To do the roundhouse kick, you need to make use of your arms to build the necessary momentum to twist your body. To start the kick, you should take a small step forward with your lead leg. As you do this, you should step with the front part of your foot while raising the balls of this foot and exposing the inner part of your lead leg, and then rotate your whole body starting with the hips to start the momentum. You only release the rear leg as the result of the momentum created by your hip and your turn. As you raise your rear leg for the kick, the leg you are standing on should skip to face backward and your rear arm should be in a straight line with the kicking leg. Practice multiple times with the bag until you are comfortable with the movements.

Knees

Knees are effective for close range attacks. In the ring, you throw your knees upward aiming for the opponent's chin, usually used with the Thai clinch to keep the head of the opponent steady. From your stance, the rear leg is the more effective knee to use. Flick your foot downward to increase the speed of your knee's ascent. After hitting the target, you should step your lead foot backward so that it will be ready to deliver another knee as the rear leg goes back down.

When doing knees make sure that your toes are pointing downward when you raise your knee.

Chapter 4: Take-downs & Take-down Defense...

There are multiple ways to take down your opponent. The details for each technique vary depending on the martial arts of origin. MMA however, allowed us to observe which ones are most effective. You can learn the fancy-looking ones from a martial arts gym with a live martial arts master. In this chapter, however, we will only teach you the most effective ones as seen in the cage.

Takedowns

Some of your opponents are not comfortable fighting on the ground. They usually avoid the ground game when they are very confident with their striking skills. You should take them out of their comfort zone by taking them down.

Double leg

The double leg take down is the most effective technique in the ring. You do this by grabbing the upper part of both legs. You should widen your stance as you reach down to their legs or you could kneel with your lead leg. An experienced fighter will widen their stance to prevent you from locking your arms. If they don't do this, you can easily lift them off the ground or push them with your torso forward. Your arms only need to prevent their legs from moving backwards. If you can do this, you will be able to take them down.

Single leg

The single leg take down is the second most effective technique. To do this, you should grab the upper part of the lead leg of your opponent. You should then lock your arms underneath the leg with your head stuck on your opponent's chest. Before your opponent can react, push him with your shoulders while lifting his lead leg high. Your goal is to take away his balance and apply a strong forward force.

Double leg trip

The third most effective way to take a man down is by using the double leg trip. You start this technique similarly with a double leg take down but you want to go down very low until your face is in the opponent's abdomen. You can do this comfortably by bending your knees and kneeling on your lead knee as you do the double leg grab. When the grip is secure, you should then use the lead foot to trip the opponent by anchoring it behind the opponent's ankle. You will be able to take them down by creating a forward motion with your torso.

Take down defense

Some fighters actually prefer to fight on the ground and do not focus too much on their striking techniques. If you think that your opponent wants to take the fight to the ground, you need to frustrate him by keeping the both of you vertical as long as possible. This is when you need to avoid their attempts to take you down through take down defense moves. Here are the basic tips to avoid getting taken down:

Know how they will take you down

If you know your opponent, you should be familiar with his favorite takedown moves. You can then train on how to counter that move.

Spread your legs

The double leg take down becomes harder to pull off if the spreads his legs apart because it prevents you from getting a good grip. Keep your stance as wide as possible without compromising your balance and you will lessen the chances of your opponent successfully using the double leg takedown.

Push the opponent's head down

In both the double leg and the single leg technique, the opponent wants to take your balance away by pushing your upper body with his torso. You can prevent his attack by pushing him down. This way, you actually direct the force of his push onto your lower body, which is a lot more stable and difficult to push.

Learn to regain your base

Your base is composed of the parts of your body that are touching the ground. When your opponent tries to take you down, they are trying to take away your base by grabbing one leg, by tripping you or by lifting you off your feet with a spinning motion. Whenever you have the opportunity to replant your feet on the ground, you should do so as soon as you can. This makes the opponent's moves futile.

Use a whizzer

A whizzer is an under-hook that you can use when your opponent has already a hold of your legs. You can do this by putting your arms under his elbow and grabbing your pants or your legs. This will make it difficult for your opponent to lift you up.

Lean forward

Most take down attempts use forward motion. To counter the forward motion, you should lean forward with your legs straight back and keeping your body straight from head to toe. Your legs will be too far away for your opponents to reach.

Anticipate the spinning and side motion

When the forward attacks don't work, the opponent tends to try to throw you sideways or to use a spinning motion to remove your base. This only works if you are not expecting them. If you think that they are about to use such an attack, side step to regain your base. You should also avoid the opponent's legs from tripping you over your knees. You can step over any trip below your knee, but you will not be able to avoid falling if the trip is above your knees.

Get back up as fast as possible

There is no better way to frustrate an opponent that has a good ground game than to get up quickly after they took you down. As soon as you realize that the take down is a success, think of ways to either get the top position or get back on your feet.

Chapter 5: The Ground Game...

Even if your opponent successfully takes you down, you need to be able to fight off your back. Your goal on the ground is to take the top position in the guard position or to minimize the damage from the bottom position. In this chapter, we will discuss the common scenarios when the fighting goes to the ground and the moves that you should use in each scenario.

The Top Position

When you take down your opponent and they end up on their back, you should take the top position as soon as possible before they can recover. You do this by placing your weight on top of the opponent either from the front or from the side. You can then deliver straight punches and hooks down to your opponent's face. You should also deliver hammer punches to frustrate your opponent and to prevent him from regaining his composure.

The Bottom Position

If you end up in the bottom, you should take the guard position as soon as possible. You do this by wrapping your legs around your opponent's abdomen. You should then control the amount of damaging strikes that your opponent can throw by pulling his head to your chest. You can do this by wrapping your arms around his neck and pulling his head against your chest. Never extend your hand towards the opponent to defend yourself. Submission artists can turn this into an opportunity for an arm bar.

Submission

You should also train on how to finish the fight with the fundamental submission moves. The submissions that are included in this book are among the most successful in MMA. You should not go into a fight looking to end it with a specific submission move. You can set up your submission moves yourself, or you take it when the opportunity presents itself.

Rear Naked Choke

The rear naked choke is the most commonly used submission technique in the ring. You usually do this when the opponent turns his back to you without defending his neck. You do the rear naked choke by slipping your dominant arm around the opponent's neck and holding your biceps of your other arm to lock the move. If the chin or the hands of the opponent doesn't interfere, you will be able to clip the opponent's jugular veins, thus cutting off the supply of oxygen to the brain. You can tighten your choke by folding and raising the elbows of your less dominant arm. You can then wrap your legs around the body of your opponent to prevent them from wriggling out of the choke.

The Guillotine

The guillotine is also a choke, but unlike the rear naked choke, the guillotine comes from the front. To do this effectively, you should have your opponent's head under your armpit. You should then clip his jugular using the forearm of the same arm. You should then use your other arm to secure the hold. You can also wrap your feet around the body of your opponent.

Chapter 6: The 7-Day MMA Boot Camp...

To learn all the fundamentals of MMA, you need a partner to help you practice. The person must also be interested in learning MMA so that you will both be enthusiastic in learning each skill. To master the fundamental skills in 7 days, you need to practice both in the mornings and the afternoons of the training day.

Day 1:

On the first day, you need to go back to all the skills discussed in the previous chapters and practice all of them with a sparring partner. You can throw kicks and punches on your own, but you will need a partner for practicing take-downs and to test you take down defense. You should practice them in the order that presented in the book. It is important that you learn the proper stance before any of other moves. You should then learn the striking skills and move on the take down and submission skills in the afternoon training.

Day 2:

If your body is not sore by the second day, you should do the following drills for striking in the morning:

Jab-Straight Combination 50 times

Jab-Straight-Hook-Uppercut Combination 50 times

Knees Training:

Grab your Partner by the neck, hold a Thai Clinch and hit him with 50 knees to the head. Have your partner stop the knees with his hands on top of each other. Change roles and train yourself to defend against knees

Do 20 roundhouse kicks and 20 spinning back kicks

It is preferable to use a heavy bag for practicing these strikes. If you don't have one, you can practice on mitts that are available in martial art shops. You can find punching mitts used in boxing and kicking mitts used in Taekwondo.

Rest for 3 minutes and do the drills again this time with the mitts.

In the afternoon, you should rest your arms and legs from punching, and focus more on takedowns, and take down defense. Try the different take down techniques suggested in the previous chapter on your partner. Take turns being the attacker and the defender. Rest when tired but get back into it after 5 minutes of resting. Top the second day by doing some 3 minute shadow boxing using your own combinations.

Day 3:

If you followed the striking drill of the previous day, you should have sore joints in your arms and feet. You should rest these parts and focus on building endurance. Here are some of the drills that you can do while resting your sore arms and legs:

Morning:

Takedowns and takedown defense training for 2 hours

Fighting on the ground training for 1 hour

Rear Naked Choke and Guillotine training for 30 minutes each

Afternoon:

Knees training 100 times

Elbows training on a punching bag 100 times

Take down and take down defense training for 2 hours

Day 4:

On the fourth day, you will test what you've learned in the 3 days of training by engaging in a sparring match with your partner. Fight in full speed but stop your punches just before hitting the other fighter's face.

Engage with full strength in take down attempts. You should also tap early when caught to avoid injuries. Do this training in both the morning and the afternoon.

Day 5:

Morning

Jab-Straight Combination 100 times with the mitts

Jab-Straight-Hook-Uppercut Combination 50 times with the mitts

Practice knees with your partner

Do 20 roundhouse kicks and 20 spinning back kicks

Take a 5-minute break and then do the same routines with an alternate stance.

Afternoon:

Do the combinations in the morning session for 3 minutes straight each. Take a minute rest in between, but get back in it immediately after. Count the number of kicks and punches that you can throw for three minutes.

Day 6:

Morning:

Take down and take down defense training for 2 hours

Fighting on the ground training for 1 hour

Rear Naked Choke and Guillotine training for 30 minutes each

Afternoon:

Knees training 100 times

Elbows training on a punching bag 100 times

Take down and take down defense training for 2 hours

Practice take down attempts for 3 minutes straight without resting. Change roles and practice again for another 3 minutes.

Do this drill until you are tired.

Day 7:

On the 7th day, you should take the morning to rest your muscles and do a full sparring session with your partner with the proper fight gear on including gloves, shin guards, head protectors and mouthpieces. Do 3 5-minute rounds in the morning and 5 5-minute rounds in the afternoon.

CONCLUSION

I hope this book was able to help you learn to master the fundamental skills of MMA.

The next step is to start and keep practicing- keep adding offensive and defensive skills to your arsenal.

Finally, if you found some value this book, then I'd like to ask you for a favor, would you be kind enough to leave a review for this book on Amazon? It'd be greatly appreciated!

Thank you and good luck!

Greg

Printed in Great Britain
by Amazon